THE GIRL WHO
TALKED TO PAINTINGS

by

Shannon K. Winston

GLASS LYRE PRESS

Design & Layout: Steven Asmussen
Cover art: "Abstract paint background" © Monstarrrr | Dreamstime.com
Author Photo: Marie-Noyale Barguirdjian

Glass Lyre Press, LLC
P.O. Box 2693
Glenview, IL 60025
www.GlassLyrePress.com

THE GIRL WHO
TALKED TO PAINTINGS

Acknowledgments & Notes

So many people have supported my writing and facilitated bringing this book into being. Thanks to my mother who read to me by candlelight—a magical experience that fueled my love of literature and poetry. Thanks, too, to my sister, who was one of my first readers. She continues to inspire me every day. I am deeply grateful to my brothers who taught me to pursue what I love. Love and gratitude to Gen, Lynkn, Tye (2006-2018), and Wyatt, who have been and continue to be integral to my happiness and to my writing life.

Blas Falconer's and Helena Mesa's friendship and encouragement of my poetry have enriched my life beyond what I ever thought possible. Because of them, I pursued my M.F.A. at Warren Wilson College—where I first conceived of this collection. I am indebted to the entire Warren Wilson Community, but especially to mentors Daisy Fried, Sandra Lim, and Alan Williamson, who taught me to be a fearless writer. This book would not have been possible without Matthew Olzmann's mentorship and steadfast belief in my project from day one. His imperative to keep writing no matter what spurred me on to find the most amazing workshops and writing communities. Diane Seuss's workshop at the Frost Place revolutionized my understanding of form. John Sibley Williams's careful reading of this manuscript was crucial in helping me think about the story this collection tells. Much gratitude, too, to Megan Pinto and Robin Rosen Chang for their friendship and thorough feedback on every poem. For their insightful comments at different stages in the process, thanks to Shannon Castleton, Carlos Andrés Gómez, Kristen Hewitt, Jill Klein, Amanda Newell, and Susan Jo Russell.

Many thanks to the Princeton Writing Program, which has supported my creative and intellectual growth at every turn. In becoming a better teacher, I have also become a better writer. I am indebted to Amanda Irwin Wilkins for encouraging me to embrace the surprise and mystery in everything I write. Thanks to my colleagues and friends, especially Adrienne Raphel and Leslie Ribovich, who always push me to revise my poems until they sing. Lauren Santangelo's steadfast friendship has been invaluable over the years as I revised and revised this collection.

A heartfelt thanks to Brian and Margie Duncan, as well as to Olga Greco, who read each line in this manuscript with great care before it went to press. I am appreciative of Marie-Noyale Barguirdjian's keen eye and infectious humor as she took my author photo. Thanks to Diane

Ardouin Creedon for her help in selecting an author photo and for her support more generally. Boundless gratitude to Ami Kaye, Steve Asmussen, Kelly Cressio-Moeller, and all the editors at Glass Lyre Press for their faith in this book. Finally, thank you to all I have undoubtedly forgotten to mention, but who have supported me and shaped this project through to publication.

Warm thanks to the following journals in which these poems have appeared, often in altered form:

A-Minor ("Collateral"), *Barren Magazine* ("Sewing"), *The Citron Review* ("Peer (n.,v.):" and "The Spinners"), *Cumberland River Review* ("After the Divorce," published as "Extractions"), *Crab Creek Review* ("Self-Portrait in White While Viewing Salvador Dalí's *Figura en una finestra*"), *Crab Orchard Review* ("Remnants"), *Dialogist* ("Upon Viewing Damien Hirst's *The Physical Impossibility of Death in the Mind of Someone Living*"), *The Inflectionist Review* ("Marbles III," published as "Marbles IV," and "In Which Self-Portraits Are Also About Others, or Ilse Bing's Musings with Her Leica Camera"), *LEON Literary Review* ("Wish Fulfillment"), *The Los Angeles Review* ("Ways to View Joan Miró's *Triptych Bleu I, II, III*," "Word Games & Space Travel," and "The Stories We Tell: Fox in a Block of Ice"), *Oxidant Engine* ("Cyanotypes"), *Plainsongs* ("Keys"), *Portland Review* ("The Girl Who Talked to Paintings"), *Pretty Owl Poetry* ("Birdcage and Shadow" and "Weston's Cabbage Always Makes Me Cry"), *RHINO Poetry* ("Notes from the Pantry, 1990"), *Small Orange Poetry Journal* ("Why He Left"), *SWWIM Every Day* ("Shame Is a Bull"), *The Tusculum Review* ("Flower Girls"), *Twyckenham Notes* ("Swallows," "The Blueprint," and "Dream of Skulls"), *Up the Staircase Quarterly* ("Stories" and "When the Speech Therapist Told Me to Say the Letter 'S'"), and *Whale Road Review* ("Palindromes").

Notes:

"Bridging the Distance" was inspired by Ira Glass's *This American Life*'s episode called "One Last Thing Before I Go" (Act I, "One Last Thing Before I Go," interview by Miki Meek) that aired on September 23, 2016.

In "The Map Snatchers," select phrases and details about the maps were taken from the Delafield Family Papers Archive (Princeton University Library).

In my research on John Singer Sargent's *Carnation, Lily, Lily, Rose* for my eponymous poem "The Girl Who Talked to Paintings," I found references to a Kate Millet as well as to different spellings of the name Katharine (with both an "a" and an "e"). I was not able to find a definitive answer about the proper spelling or verify that they were the same person. I thus decided to play up this ambiguity in the poem.

The inspiration for my poem, "Dream of Skulls," was a *Rattle* Ekphrastic Challenge from December 2018 that featured an untitled photograph by Kari Gunter-Seymour.

"I am out with lanterns, looking for myself."
—Emily Dickinson

"[T]here is a reflexivity of the sensible; the mirror translates and reproduces that reflexivity . . . Everything that is most secret about me passes into that face, that flat, closed being of which I was already dimly aware, from having seen my reflection mirrored in water."
—Maurice Merleau-Ponty, "Eye and Mind"

CONTENTS

VANTAGE POINTS

BY A DIFFERENT NAME

A First Draft, A Sketch

Solitude Leaves Its Own Kind of Mark

Spheres Unlock Other Spheres

Hard to See, Harder to Name

To Get a Better Look

Blueprints

Ways to View Joan Miró's
Triptych Bleu I, II, III

Start with the left,
and you'll see rain on
a windshield after a storm.

Begin with the right,
and you'll see only a kite string
drifting against the sky.

There are a thousand
ways to begin a story.
With the middle, perhaps,

is best: with a red sewing
needle stitching up black holes.
Or maybe they aren't

holes but pebbles
skimming the water
seconds before they sink.

There are also a million ways
to interpret a story.
The way I took my lover's

silence for indifference.
The way she thought
my idle chatter was irreverence.

The way I sometimes
thought my sneaking to
her house in the middle

of the night was so lonely—
our secret rendezvous
collecting like black dots

against a blue canvas.
But then again,
how lovely the snow fell

all around me as I
trekked back and forth
between her house

and mine at midnight.
The sidewalk appeared
like black ovals

beneath my feet
where the snow
had melted. These

tiny openings.
How easy silence seemed.
Chosen, not imposed.

Like something
I could lean into,
like a simple red sliver.

A blot of paint.
To embroider, decorate.
To strip back, cut.

Yes, maybe
this is the best
way in.

∞

VANTAGE POINTS

Self-Portrait in White While Viewing Salvador Dalí's *Figura en una finestra*

Like me, Dalí hid his grievances
in the hem of a girl's dress,

in the thick, blue stripes
running down her back.

In art they call mistakes
or amendments

mid-stroke *pentimento*.
I call them silence:

Nine years old, I'm sitting
by my father on the front

porch watching
lightning slice the sky.

We've run out
of things to say.

Me, his greatest regret:
a daughter, not a son.

Him, mine. A father
I could no longer talk to.

If grief were a color,
it would be white. I'm sure of it.

The girl in the painting
leans against the windowsill.

What was she thinking?
The window opens

onto the Mediterranean,
a sailboat, and mountains.

In the glass pane,
I glimpse the reflection

of a small white house
in the distance.

If only I could step through
the canvas, climb out

the window, and over waves
to this threshold.

I would turn the brass
doorknob and feel

my way through this strange,
yet not altogether unfamiliar, space

as my father recedes
into the background.

I would call the girl, sister.
This place, my home.

Marbles I

In the distance,
a man pulls

a ball
as small as

a marble.
Up close

it morphs into
a balloon

double his size.
Blue-green.

How hard
it must be

to carry the world
through the world—

A Straight Line

I'm not asking you for the moon—
a teacher reprimanded me. I couldn't draw

a straight line. Even with a ruler,
my hands shook. Instead, I made a river

curved with flowers and boats.
I forgot about the moon.

When I played ring-around-the-rosy,
I never saw a rose.

I skipped around and around
as if circling a void.

Bridging the Distance

Andrew Wyeth, *Widow's Walk*

Surely, this is as close
as we'll ever get to flying.

Or maybe not.
Maybe widows' walks are

more like phone booths
high up in the sky

where you go to call the dead.
In Otsuchi, Japan, mourners trek uphill

to a garden where Itaru Sasaki
placed a disconnected rotary phone

inside a glass phone booth.
How was your day?

a child asks her grandfather
as she looks out to sea.

What did you have for dinner?
a woman asks her lover.

Her breath fogs the glass where
she traces his face with her fingers.

Multiple Exposures: A Study

Berenice Abbott, *Multiple Exposure of a Swinging Ball*

White balls sail
through darkness

    like miniature moons,

like salt skirting
a silver spoon.

    How easy motion looks

from this vantage point.
But just today, a blue jay—

    thwarted by transparency—

flew straight into my window.
I heard a thud, looked up:

not even a smudge.
The bird must've swung around,

    stunned, and reversed course. But I pressed

my hand against the glass anyway,
hoping to feel something.

Swallows

Swallows
       on telephone wires
always remind me

       of clothespins. Their
shoulders and wings
       form the grooves.

The springs: the heart—
       although from
a different angle,

       these birds
resemble minute
       marks on a clock,

as if time could be
       stretched out
on a line like so—

       Yes, I can almost
picture it: a screen
       projecting memories

I wish I'd had,
       but were never
mine.

A yellow boat.
       A lake. A teenage daughter
and her father.

       How silently
they glide through water,
       which swallows their

every gesture.
        He paddles on the left,
she on the right

        in perfect
synchronicity. She smiles
        as sunlight

tickles her dimples
        and skims his
graying hair.

        Above them,
leaves carve blue
        shapes from the sky,

air, and water.
        So, too, do their oars.
One stroke is

        curved like a bird;
one is straight
        like a wire in the waves

of memory.
        Every slice is even
and sure, the way

        their love
chisels but never cuts
        too close to bone.

The Stories We Tell: Fox in a Block of Ice

I shouldn't,
but I find it beautiful—

the way its paws lift
slightly as if still

clawing the air.
Its yellow fur

somehow softer,
more vulnerable

pressed against ice
which amplifies

its body like
a magnifying glass:

the spots on its back,
the black fur

around its neck.
This is as close as

I will ever get
to surrender.

Except its face
is submerged

in cracks too thick
to see through.

As if the river that
froze it also wanted

to protect it from
those who would later

marvel at it,
forgetting,

as I do,
that it's not just

a piece of art.
I lean in closer

as if looking for
a story I can learn from—

one about cold
temperatures,

difficult crossings,
eyes that never shut.

Marbles II

two marbles nested

                    [...]

                                        inside Russian dolls

clunk!! clunk!! clunk!!

                    [...]

                                        a heartbeat

one teal, one blue

                    [...]

                                        rain

like seeds

                    [...]

                                        more like an echo

tap, tap, tap!!!

                    [...]

                                        a whisper, a giggle

a thousand wings

                    [...]

                                        knifing the air

orbiting a second

[...]

more perfect set of eyes

∞

By a Different Name

Sewing

a blue button, a handkerchief, a strand of hair. when i was a child, my grandmother would praise my sister's discerning eyes as if her observations made her more capable & worthy of love. so i set out to see more sharply, to take in the things of this world: the curve of a keyhole, a doorframe, a water glass. all the shapes that contain us. afraid of missing the slightest detail, i sewed my observations into a piece of fabric i folded & stored under my pillow. this is what dreams are made of: a hairclip, a chipped cup, a worry doll. weaving in & out, out & in, my needle pierced & wove & bound letters against letters until words emerged against the backdrop of my blue fabric. a G to an O to an N. later came the E. what i hadn't anticipated was the numbness, the small pricks in my fingers as letters formed & deformed under my touch. what i hadn't anticipated was the way objects lost & regained their shape. G O N E. what i hadn't anticipated was the pleasure & the pain i felt until i tethered what i loved, until it couldn't move.

Why He Left

I don't know. I invent so many stories about my father.
I was left on a doorstep, in an open-air market, in a department
store with a Post-it: *Love her, give her water,*

as if I were a plant. Perhaps he was a prince, a tailor,
a train conductor who gave chocolates to everyone in his compartment.
What do I know? I invent so many stories. About my father:

yes, maybe he had to go? Maybe before
leaving he showed me chameleons, blood moons, and other wonderment.
A Post-it note left by a blooming orchid—*Love, give it water.*

Her roots will grow deep. Maybe there were also orangutans and sea otters
between us. Or maybe he had other more important appointments?
How often I've been told that I don't need a father.

Still, each night I studied how to be a good daughter.
Now etymologies offer me something more cogent.
Take *deracination,* from *de* + *racine* (root), penned on a Post-it note far from love and wate

Cut off at the stems, my orchid splintered the way the meaning of *de* fractures
into *from* and *opposing forces.* Alone in my apartment,
I invert so many stories: about my father, about strangers.
I scribble on Post-it notes, turn them into boats, set them adrift in water.

The Spinners

Early on, I learned how to put a spin on things—
        something I picked up from the spinners in my hometown.

Me, the quiet observer who watched artisans
        at fairs and in storefront windows turn batting,

spool by spool, into fine, magnificent strands.
        Magenta, turquoise, purple—the seamlessness of it all.

A luscious tapestry I yearned to dive into. I wove the most eloquent deceptions.
        There are just too many guys to choose from.

He's an economist who travels for work. How carefully I tucked away
        the strands that might betray me.

I haven't found the right man, I told the vendor at the market
        who asked about my family while selling me soap in purple wax paper.

Some lies, too, were beautiful in their half-truths: *No, she's just a good friend.*
        I cherished those the most. *She gave me a key so I could check on the plants.*

More and more, my words tangled in all the wrong places, when I blushed
        too much or smiled too little. When I was caught

circling a block in a neighborhood that wasn't mine. *My husband.*
        Too many guys. Right man. Friend. I tripped

on invisible spools. Love: a plush knotted turquoise. At night,
        after cleaning away the lies, I reclined on wax paper

and wove a tapestry syllable by magenta syllable,
        hoping it would sustain my weight.

Peer (n.,v.):

When you say *peer*, I hear *pear*. I think of the day in late August when I pulled over and snuck into a stranger's backyard to steal fruit right off the tree. I left three seeds in recompense. Somehow, the trade seemed equivalent. The way I substitute an "a" for an "e" or an "i." *Peer, pear, pair.* The way I rearrange a phrase until it becomes another: *read paper, appear dear.* Things work this way, too. An almond: a pendant. Blue canvas: a strip of the sea. A hand: the state of Michigan. *Appear dear.* Your face, too, reminds me of someone I once loved. Please understand, then, why I call you by a different name.

The Map Snatchers

They'd steal maps from almost anywhere:
tourist shops, museums, library archives,
even off friends' dining room walls.
They looked innocent enough: these two
women in their mid-forties pretending to be
just friends. They had long figured
out how to render themselves invisible.
Some maps they wrapped in napkins,
others they folded into coin purses.
Be good wives, gentle mothers,
their families urged, pushing their
books aside and whisking them off
to finishing school. *Proper women
don't become geologists or cartographers.*
Even as they poured over latitudes
and longitudes, they never touched.
Instead, they'd whisper their findings
to one another. *Interior parts,*
a map of Lake Superior read,
Topographies Bureau, Sept 2, 1826.
Creased paper softened in their hands.
Around the Great Lakes, a faint red crayon
and black dots threaded
Naples I to *Belle Isle* to *Isle Royale*
and back again in a collarbone shape.
Did it give them some comfort
that centuries of women had slipped out
to meet in the park? Did they, too, hide
newspaper clippings and articles
in recipe books to share with one another?
They tucked their love of adventure
into the hems of their skirts, smiling
as they moved from their kitchens
to their dining rooms and back again.

But sometimes, when exhausted,
they'd close their eyes
and imagine themselves far out
on a sandbar away from it all—
laughing and diving into water so blue
and vast it opened onto uncharted spaces,
glinting, like them, with limestone and lake.

Cyanotypes

For Anna Aktins, botanist and the first female photographer

Slippery, wet algae

uprooted

from the sea

A slow emerging

of absences & presences

Fucus nodosus,

strange syllables

on my tongue

In darkness,

my hands: how they burn with

ferric ammonium,

Some people peer into the sky,

for the smallest sketches

It all hinges on patience—

shadows. Let's let the light through

Let's expose the inner workings

of chemistry

of ourselves

Let's turn the whole world blue—

dangle like pearls

like unclasped necklaces

white imprints on salt paper.

of negative & positive

skeletal forms aglow.

Furcellaria fastigiata—

surface

brilliant, biting, scaly—

phosphorescence, too, congeals in

starlike constellations,

and the finest lines.

I sink down into waves

of the infinite.

let's peel back the

separations of leaf and vein.

of bone, body, muscle

to uncover how little

we truly know.

let it all burst forth

and expose our breath: animated by

nearly undetectable   sunrays.

∞

A First Draft, A Sketch

The Girl Who Talked to Paintings

For Katharine Millet, the original subject of
John Singer Sargent's *Carnation, Lily, Lily, Rose*

1.

She's long gone, but I always look for her:
the girl Sargent buried in paint. Like dirt,
each brush stroke covered her dark, knotted hair.
Greens blotted out the patterns in her skirt.
Her asymmetrical smile and fire eyes:
he erased those too. And the eczema,
her knocked knees. Sargent wanted fireflies,
lanterns, a garden with a soft aura.
How her chest buckled under the pastels.
How her body was heavy with lilies,
roses, and carnations. *Be a bluebell,
be a good girl. Smile. Be sure to say please.*
Katharine, Catherine, or was it Kate?
I, too, was a first draft, a sketch, half-baked.

2.

I, too, was a first draft, a sketch, half-baked.
A girl with angled teeth and a wet lisp:
all of my life I've felt like a mistake.
The girl in school no one wanted to kiss.
My parents fought and fought about my name,
as if unsure they wanted me at all.
They only agreed on my middle name:
Katherine with a "K." *What a sweet doll—*
words no one ever said. Tubes and wires
keeping preemie me alive. *Robot girl,
here's a lantern. A matchstick. Light a fire.*
I smiled. My grandmother gave me her pearls.
I said *thank you.* When they chipped: *I'm sorry.*
And this is only part of the story.

3.

And this is only part of the story.
Stroke by stroke, Sargent painted two sisters
in Katharine's place: Polly and Dolly.
Petal-smooth skin, ruffled dresses, flowers
waiting to be plucked as one might a rose.
Give them lanterns. These props propped up by props.
Turn their heads just so. *Yes, girls, keep this pose.*
The way, in college, I got all made up
for boys I'd never love. Foundation, rouge,
lipstick: each day I picked a different way
to transform myself. I wore rings and huge
hoop earrings. *Make me better. Make me good.*
Be good. The soundtrack of my childhood.

4.

Be good. The soundtrack of my childhood:
Be better. Would my father love me then?
What had I done wrong? Said? Tell me, what had . . . ?
I scanned each day for my mistakes: five, ten,
twenty, thirty times. Something I had said
made my father scream. Curled on the floor,
I pulled at the strings of my old bedspread.
Be good. I was his curious daughter
who dared to ask about his new "best friend,"
about flowers, his wedding, his new wife.
Who said, *But I thought Mom was your best friend?*
And how much did he spend on his new life?
My nickname in school: nosy rosy. *Girl,*
be quiet. Sit pretty with your fake pearls.

5.

I sat so quietly in my fake pearls—
when my father left, when my mother cried.
When I burned myself with a hair curler.
When I crashed my first bike trying to fly,
and blood trickled between my legs. *She's lost
her womanhood,* my aunt cried on the phone.
For days, I sat in a warm bath. At last,
I went back to school and then everyone
asked: *What happened to you?* I got quiet.
A decade later, in a swimsuit store
in Nice a clerk said that I wasn't quite
right. I had such a flat chest. *A doctor.
You must see one soon.* In the fitting room:
gold, pink, and black suits. Each one a costume.

6.

Yes, Sargent's girls, too, wear costumes. Each one
in a dress (nightgown?) to match the lilies.
The white ruffles itched their skin, the lanterns'
glow chafed their hands. Their legs cramped. How early
they learned beauty's stringent cost of entry.
Or maybe not. Maybe the saleswomen
flocked to them with rose perfume and bracelets
and Mary Janes. *Try x, y, and z. Then
model for us. What sweet girls, dolls. Yes, tilt
your heads just so.* Maybe they soaked it up.
But what do they do when no one's around?
Do they drop their dolls and chip china cups?
What would they say if the painting had sound?

Do they trace their own shadows on a wall?
Like me, do they whisper: *No,*

that's not me
at all?

7.

No, that's not her. No. Once, I got so close
to Sargent's *Carnation, Lily, Lily,*
Rose, I saw only globs of paint. I froze
before sticky reds. A security
guard in the Tate Museum shooed me back.
Not before I soaked in the thick yellows,
and swirly greens. Not before I could ask:
You in there? Katharine, Catherine, or Kate?
Not before I saw a gooey white dot,
a few dried cracks, and a rash upward brush
stroke. *Did you slip through the uneven spots?*
Up close, everything sags or turns to mush
or becomes something else entirely.
The way pruning and taming stand in for
      love. The way love is confused with beauty.
      The way Sargent is and is not my father.

∞

SOLITUDE LEAVES ITS OWN KIND OF MARK

An Artist at Her Drawing Board

At first it was
unrecognizable:

this charcoal
mark. Like a fine

line, a telephone wire
where a single

bird perches.
One more stroke

made a strand
of hair, a curl,

a woman's profile.
The nape of her

neck, the shadow
of her cheek.

Sometimes,
the process is slow;

sometimes it's so fast
it's easy to miss

the instant
in which a body

takes shape in
white draft paper.

It's easy to blur
a nose or a grin with

overeager hands.
But when I feel

the contours of a face,
an elbow, or a nail,

I linger longer,
hoping

to glimpse
the woman who

once appeared
before me.

Before I could reach
out to touch her,

she receded
as if she had never

been there.
Solitude leaves

its own kind of mark:
uneven, yes,

and wider than
a pinky finger.

Birdcage and Shadows

Imogen Cunningham, *photograph*

Imagine your loneliness
is a room with shadows

of leaves projected onto
whitewashed walls.

It's easier for you
to picture your feelings

cinematically, to project
them outside

of yourself and watch
them reel by.

As if they never belonged
to you, as if someone

else has trouble finding her
footing in the world.

My hands are cold,
you replied, when a man

said he loved you. Or,
I'm not sure I understand

the question, when a friend
asked what you desired most.

Project, from *proicere,*
to expel or abandon.

In this room, there's an empty
birdcage with bent bars.

Did the bird, like you,
try to hurl itself out

of this domestic scene
in search of something

else to care for?
Look, in the foreground,

there's an outline of a boy.
If you had been more

maternal, you might have
loved him—his rounded

cheeks, his soft nose.
Yes, that might have been enough.

Collateral

The highway cuts
through town after small town,
farmland unfolding
in my rearview mirror
like a paper fan.

\\

Leaves blur into fine green dots
as I drive farther and farther
from the only place I've ever called home.

\\

Outside my car window, birds
stitch up a resting place. Branch by branch.

\\

A girl hugs a ragdoll
in the seat of a passing van.
Her mother throws
her arms into the air.
Her father sits
behind the steering wheel
and shouts.
Or is he laughing?

\\

As a child, I glimpsed my parents
behind half-closed doors:
an arm wave, a fist against
a door. *Never . . . Stop it!*
Try to take care. Their voices rose

higher and higher.
Your daughter.
Me, in a corner, trying
not to make a sound,
trying to read their lips.
Trying, but unable,
to look away.

Over the radio, a note,
a pause, then static.

\\

My mother used to
press her index finger
to her lips:
sssshhhh, sssshhhh.
To please her,
I stuffed my mouth
with air.

\\

Quiet. Hush hush.
Sssshhhh, sssshhhh.
If *sssshhhh* were a shape,
what shape would it be?
S-shaped skid marks skim
across the asphalt in front of me.
Charcoal lines
thicken in the curves.

The road becomes a piece of draft paper.

I try to conjure images
of my mother and father.
But only words,
then letters appear.
I string them together
as best I can.

\\

Two seashells clank, one inside
the other, in my cupholder.
Pressing one up to my ear,
I want to hear
the ocean, but all I hear
is *sssshhhh, sssshhhh*—

                                        Hush, hush,
                              my father cautioned:

                                        you say too much.
                              The light was knife-like

                                        under the door
                                            as it closed

                                        behind him
                                    for the last time.

\\

The wind rustles
the cornstalks to my left.
How seamlessly they shift,
like the finest threads
in the yellow blanket
that kept me warm at night
amid the windmills and lakes.

\\

At dusk, headlines glint like ellipses.
Only the hum of the car engine
punctuates the quiet.
I drive deeper
and deeper into silence.

Marbles III

Inside, red-orange
strands unfurl
like the light
that sutures
earth to sky.
Me, this moment, this morning:
all threaded together
as if it were that easy—

Flower Girls

John Singer Sargent, *Polly Barnard,*
Study for "Carnation, Lily, Lily, Rose"

After the ceremony our father whisked us away,
dropped us off in a parking lot on the side of the highway
before returning to the reception.

We waited (seconds? minutes?
hours?) for our mother to pick us up.
Heat lightning ripped through the sky

as semis whirred past us,
stirring up plastic bags and cigarette butts
at our feet. Standing perfectly still,

we resembled old dolls
stowed away, brushed seamlessly
into my father's past.

Our best thrift store dresses
clung to our stomachs. Sweat curved into
crescent moons under our arms,

where threads frayed.
How we had stepped down the aisle
just hours before with white lilies.

We had scattered them slowly, feeling
each petal slip through our fingertips, as if
we were offering up a small part of ourselves.

Years later, in the Tate Museum,
I gazed at Sargent's *Carnation, Lily, Lily, Rose*
and suddenly recalled that night.

How I wished I had leaned over
and whispered to my sister: *Close your eyes,*
you be Lily, I'll be Rose.

If only we'd had our own
makeshift lanterns into which we could
have thrown bottle caps,

gum wrappers, and glass.
We would have watched it all smolder.
We would have transformed

the parking lot into our own garden
where cut flowers find new roots
and girls like us are given a second chance.

∞

Spheres Unlock
Other Spheres

View (n.,v.):

As a child, in my grandmother's bathroom, I spun a hand mirror round and round. As its metal arm pivoted, I saw a half-open door, a watering can, a splintered wooden fence. Sometimes, I'd spin the mirror slowly. Rotation by rotation: the thick orange fibers in a hand towel, a frayed hair in the sink, a crack in the wall. Or I'd spin the mirror so fast that objects galloped: the soap dish jumped, the clothesline puckered, flamingos sashayed across the plastic shower curtain. Was I turning the mirror or was it turning me? Sunflowers swayed in the wallpaper. My profile half in, half outside the frame. My body cleaved.

Marbles IV

A marble pushed
through a keyhole.

The keyhole turned
pendant,

turned inverted
exclamation point,

turned
chess pawn,

turned
telescope—

And just like that,
spheres

unlock
other spheres.

Keys

More than the art deco tables,
      the zebra print chairs,
the lamps shaped like stage lights,

      I come to the antique shop week
after week for the old keys. Tucked away in
      a cardboard box, rusted

and misshapen, of no use anymore.
      Most customers ignore them
or brush them off as junk.

      But in each key, I see an untold story,
a small part of me: my wariness
      in a blunted bit, my hesitance

in the dip of a collar—
      the metal piece just after
the stem and before

      the throat. This is also
where my secrets lodge—
      in the soft folds of my larynx.

Each move in and out, out and in
      of a lock wielded by frustrated
loving, impatient hands.

      But me: I always take my time.
Once, I held a key up to the store window
      to let a tunnel of light shine

through. The wave-like indentations
      of the bow transformed
the outside world into a sea.

All around me, salt and algae.
Key, from the Spanish *cayo*, meaning shoal or reef.
And suddenly, I was swimming

with the woman next to me who had once
lent me her books. As she did, her sleeve
slipped and revealed a pond-shaped

birthmark on her wrist.
No, it's an estuary. In the water, her cap
bobbed up like a sparrow against the sky.

If I had been braver,
I would have loved her—

Word Games & Space Travel

Michael Thompson, *Girl with a Hole in Her Stocking*

A hesitation. A hole. A rip.
      Sometimes, my thoughts

proceed like this. Like a teasing
      at the seams where one

thread loosens, then another,
      only to contract elsewhere.

The way I think *splinter,*
      then *sister.* O, the association

games she and I played
      to pass the time. *Fall,*

she'd say. *Trampoline,* I'd reply.
      Corkscrew, curls.

Syllables stitched up
      the hours. *Almond, eye,*

telescope. What do you see?
      A blue earring lost

in the baseboards. Through our
      games, it morphed into

a blueberry, a raindrop, a lake big
      enough to swim in.

What do you feel? Felt, cloth, velvet.
      My tongue explored

each word, probing the space
      between letters.

Space: a blank. *To space*: to forget.
   Outer Space. Me and my sister:

two astronauts tasked
   with discovering dark matter,

big dippers, Orion's Belt.
   All of it hidden in a "C"

or an "O," galaxies nestled
   in unsuspecting letters.

Even now, my fingers pick
   at snags in my nylons

and pull and pull—
   Unravel. Gravel. Travel.

To glimpse what lies
   beneath, behind, beyond.

Remnants

Tourne, pousse, plie—three words
my mother taught me while kneading dough.

Bent over the counter like Vermeer's astronomer,
I traced star shapes in the flour.

Turn, push, fold. The foreign assemblage
of words rose on my tongue.

Tourne, pousse, plie. My mother sprinkled water
on the counter as white light filtered

through the kitchen window. *Turn, push, fold*—
air bubbles nested in yeast, burst like comets.

The oven's pale-yellow coils bluing.
Rock, dust, ice.

The heating and cooling
and reheating of particles in the making.

∞

HARD TO SEE,
HARDER TO NAME

Forgetting My French

Sometimes,
    I stand before

the mirror
    and curse how

easily I forget
    the word

for "light."
    No, it's not

lumière,
    a word that's far

too bright for
    what I'm trying

to describe.
    This sunlight

falls more nimbly,
    as if through

the dusty screen
    of my half-open

eyes when I wake
    unsure where

I am. Or when
    I make careless

mistakes:
    confusing *lueur,*

glow, with
        fleurs, flowers.

In spring,
        magnolia petals

scatter on
        the sidewalk

like tiny
        upturned hands.

Their tissue,
        a soft white

tinged with
        a pink that's

hard to see
        and even

harder
        to name.

When the Speech Therapist Told Me to Say the Letter "S," I Opened My Mouth

and nothing.

I tried again. Nothing.

Nothing. A thorn wedged
between my teeth. Beauty's sharpest edge.

I've always fumbled over the most basic tasks. Again and again,
my tongue rubbed until it bled.

Try to say your name, she urged.

Say anything.

Notes from the Pantry, 1990

1.

There was Clorox and darkness.

2.

Strawberry and blueberry preserves in mason jars, too. One stacked on top of the other.

3.

Crackers and marbles. A deck of cards.

4.

It was like being in a Joseph Cornell box. My favorite, his *Pharmacy, 1943:* a cabinet of medicine jars arranged 5 down, 4 across.

5.

Separate containers for a pink candy wrapper, a yellow butterfly wing, a seashell, a small painted city on curled paper.

6.

Maybe there was also a feather and coral. I'm not sure.

7.

Or perhaps it was olives and cranberries.

8.

Tenses, too, must be stored separately.

9.

Always, this scene returns on repeat: me, in the pantry, searching for the vacuum. My father appears suddenly in the doorframe.

10.

An egg, a branch, newspaper clippings.

11.

As if whispering into a confessional, he says: I have another wife and soon a son.

12.

Don't tell your mother.

13.

Water chestnuts, purple ribbon, flower seeds.

14.

My sticky hands let go of the vacuum.

15.

Just ten, I wondered: Could I bottle this secret?

16.

Leave it here, in this box of boxes.

17.

Hula-hoops, tweezers, fake pearls.

18.

My father slips salt and a miniature scale into my palm.

19.

Close your eyes. Hold fast these parting gifts:

20.

Anger, a Tarot card, despair, two painted quail eggs.

Marbles V

I cherish their slow,
hesitant rolls

and wobbles
across the floor

the most.
It's something

about their
deliberate

trajectory toward
an uncertain

destination
that reminds me

of myself.
Is this how

my mother felt,
watching me walk

for the first time?
One foot, then ...

then the other.
Each step its own

miracle after all
those months

in the hospital.
Or did she feel only fear

as she whispered:
Will she make it

to the other side
of the room?

Dream of Skulls

Kari Gunter-Seymour, *Untitled*

No one taught me how
　　　　to handle fragile things:

the lone egg on
　　　　the countertop

that glistened
　　　　like a polished skull

or the one-inch worry
　　　　dolls made of sticks

that cracked like bones
　　　　under my pillow,

where I placed the tooth
　　　　that would not

give, would not yield
　　　　until finally it did.

When I held a baby
　　　　for the first time,

I wanted nothing
　　　　more than to give

him back, afraid my fingers,
　　　　curious and eager,

might slip into the soft
　　　　spot in his head,

might press
　　　　a little too hard.

Each ridge tender,
       ripe as the sweetest

peach. Its center: a pit
       tinged crimson.

The trace of where
       lips had once been.

∞

To Get a Better Look

Stories

a woman placed her baby

in a basket and sent it downriver

with a blanket and two coins

talismans for safe passage

nothing about this is real

doctors said a week or two at most

lungs collapse like matchsticks

there were no other options

maybe there's more to the story

a woman, a baby, a river

arrange the details so they matter

mud beneath her feet

did she lean in to whisper:

I dreamed there was no baby

just a box of basil and cardamom

a woman put snapdragons

in a box under her bed

with basil and cardamom

amulets for richer dreams

everything about this is real

doctors are only for the weak

lungs radiate with matchstick light

there are always options

maybe that's all there is to it

a woman, snapdragons, a dreamer

arrange the details willy-nilly

plum carpet under her toes

did she lean in to whisper:

I dreamed I was sent downriver

in a basket with a blanket

Weston's Cabbage Always Makes Me Cry

Edward Weston, *Cabbage Leaf*

It's something about
the way the leaf
droops onto the floor.

The gelatin silver:
black on black. I want
to console it. To lift

up its leaves, to heal
the spot where a vein
broke. This is not about

personification,
although some days
the cabbage looks like

a crumpled prom
dress, which makes me
wonder where the girl

who wore it has gone.
Does she even
remember this dress?

The one she put on
layaway and later bought
with a jar full of coins?

To most, the fabric's white
flocking resembled flowers,
but to her they were birds.

Big, whooshing all
around her, they lifted her
higher and higher

above the dance floor,
transforming her
clumsiness and shyness

into confident grace:
This is what love must feel like,
she thought, twirling.

Love, like the distant
flapping of wings
against blue taffeta.

I had watched her dance.
Watched shadows skirt
the wall as she threw

her arms over her head—
a gesture of joy or drowning;
I could not tell which.

Even now, looking at Weston's
photograph years later,
I wonder:

Were those birds
detaching themselves,
stitch by stitch from her dress,

sinking their beaks
into the ripest, most tender
part of her flesh?

Upon Viewing Damien Hirst's *The Physical Impossibility of Death in the Mind of Someone Living*

Whether the shark is flying
      through the air

or swimming in
      water, it's hard to tell.

In death,
      anything's possible.

The shark's mouth
      is wide open as if

in protest. If it had a voice,
      it would be screaming.

Although, maybe death is as
      silent as this glass box,

which holds the unknown
      with a transparent

ease. How finite
      the world seems. I look into

the shark's tank and try to see
      what tomorrow contains.

I can't picture it.
      Both wanting and not

to contemplate it,
      I crouch down

to get a better look, to gaze
        deeper into the shark's jaws. Is it better

to see my reflection
        or nothing at all?

∞

BLUEPRINTS

Wish Fulfillment

Paul Klee, *Pink Spring in Deep Winter*

Spectacular: the way pink petals open
        against an equally pink
sky. Each brush stroke: a stem

        that connects to other stems,
to fine lines, and blooming buds.
        If I look closely,

I see a map, cracked
        glass, and tiny veins.
The blueprint of my own clumsy

        body, too, projected onto the clouds.
My ribs, my crooked teeth, the scar
        on my right cheek.

My hard, unassuming breasts.
        My legs, bruised from
knocking into objects

        I forget are there.
On the canvas, struggle becomes
        grace: awkwardness its own

kind of beauty. Here where
        even the warmest hues
bloom from snow.

        A single crocus muscles
its way into open air:
        past bark, thorn, and rock.

Past ice and mud. Its bud
        no bigger than a clenched
fist. Its undersides crimson

—a color I so often
confuse with the body's
          vibrant contusions.

After the Divorce

On our hands and knees,
my mother and I ripped up
the orange shag carpet

in our new apartment.
Peeling back foam and mold,
we groped our way to wood.

Above me, a poster
of Gustave Caillebotte's
Les raboteurs de parquet.

Three men hunched over
while sanding a hardwood floor.
How I admired their chiseled

backs, their nimble exertion,
this whittling the body
down to its joints.

Do you only teach your sons your trade?
I asked them, as if I, too,
were in the scene, slightly offstage.

I brushed away the shavings
that curled like tendrils
at my feet, then reached

for sandpaper, a hammer,
and nails. For the strongest instruments
with which to dismantle the layers

and begin anew. As I scraped back
the layers, my ligaments burned.
Ligament, from *ligare*: to bind, to tie.

To hold captive, but also to cohere.
I bore into the floor
again and again.

Shame Is a Bull

Vladimir Fokanov, *Girl Carrying Bull*

I carry the bull on my shoulders.
Some days the weight is impossible:

its skull bores into my collar,
sweat pools under my arms

and trickles around my breasts.
My first words: not *yes* or *please*,

but *no, my way, never.*
I want, I want . . .

Other days, delight burns
in my legs, my arms ache

as I hoist this beast through
the void, across rivers

and sandbars, over snowcapped
mountains, through galaxies.

My muscles, its muscles
burned and buoyed by gravity.

And always the trembling
of my body, our bodies

on the brink—
Only when we reach a clearing,

do we turn to one another
in some gesture of self-recognition,

do I glimpse my reflection
in its iris. My flickering self-portrait.

With my mouth pressed
up against its soft, dank ear,

I insist: *The only way
through is through*—

The Blueprint

Edward Hopper, *Girl at Sewing Machine*

Those who saw her day after day
never once asked what she was
thinking. If they had, they would
have stepped into a world
where lavender captures
memories, wood and nails conjure
regret, and apple blossoms
are signs of the future.
Some days, cotton was the color
of yellow paint; at other times,
it tasted like macarons. Foolish,
careless, ridiculous girl.
*You'll be a good wife, an even
better mother,* her mother dreamed
up for her. *You'll be an accountant
or a lawyer,* her father urged.
She nodded and smiled.
Behind her, light cast shadows
in the shapes of tunnels
that threaded through moss-
covered cities to the bluest
estuaries, to houses stitched
with ivory and burdock root,
to hummingbirds weaving
archways and bridges out of air.
Glass and thread were her starting points.
The window frame was a foundation.
She would build from there.

Glimpse (n.,v.):

In a bent fork, I see a part in an old man's hair. Where the tines curve, a sliver of air and scalp. In an orange peel, a down pillow. Does it matter that I don't see the laundry piling up? I never clean the bottom of my charred frying pan. Like two explorers, my index and middle fingers leave their prints on its Mars-like surface. My violin collects dust in the closet. *Why aren't you playing?* my mother would ask. Behind closed doors, I'd press my right eye up to the violin's f-holes. Light funneled through curved slats the way sunlight spirals through a cave. I wandered through the violin's cool depths for hours. And when my sister pointed out a crack in our bedroom window, behind the rusted, moldy blinds, behind our loneliness and despair, I said: *That's not a crack, it's a map.*

Palindromes

Out on the Port Townsend Ferry, I watched
seagulls rise, then dip along the horizon.

Two men warred over chess as a girl twirled
in a blue polka-dotted dress: a woman in a sunhat

skimmed a book with pages so thin
I thought I could see right through them,

could see each letter reflecting back
at me in the saltwater in the midday sun.

Saw spelled backwards is *was.*
Noon spelled backwards is *noon.*

Some things are harder to name.
My love—what I never dared

call my lover who I kissed
behind the azaleas in the park.

Fumbling through her blouse,
I touched the fault line just north

of a north, past the seesaw
and monkey bars, where desire resides.

Chair, in French, means flesh.
Fear inverted is nonsense.

But *level* spelled backwards is level.
Dust unfolded at eye level

as we touched.
Her skin was wet with dew

and shadows of upturned leaves.
Boat-shaped, they slid over us,

casting silhouettes
in the tenderest spots:

between joint, muscle, bone.
Reprise: again.

Une reprise: a mend.
Again and again,

our hands searched out loss
and gave it sails,

then watched
it drift from view.

In Which Self-Portraits Are Also About Others, or Ilse Bing's Musings with Her Camera About Photography

Ilse Bing, *Self-Portrait in Mirrors*

Impossible. How can we ever fit

into the same picture if we

that stumble forth, awkward and unsure? We

like the way light filters through

in our bodies—

like microscopic miracles

let's zoom in.

Let's be the projector and the screen.

we see ourselves

In the center of this photograph

one eye pressed into the lens,

one eye gazing sidelong

captures it all

—heart, scar

against the camera flash

In these passageways

we try to make ourselves whole

strong as before

all these pieces of ourselves

are nothing but reflections

leave only the smallest traces,

the escape routes

veins, tiny inlets

trembling before us;

Let's examine the particles.

The camera and the eye. Can

better now?

I sit with

a hand cupped over my ear

the mirror in the foreground

reflects our image back to us

love, loss—

in the crossings of glass, metal, flesh.

angels brush up against us

again and again

only stranger. Other.

About the Author

Shannon K. Winston holds an M.F.A. in poetry from Warren Wilson College and a Ph.D. in Comparative Literature from the University of Michigan—Ann Arbor. She has previously published *Threads Give Way* (Cold Press Publishing, 2010). Her poems have appeared in *RHINO, Crab Creek Review, The Citron Review, The Los Angeles Review, Zone 3,* and elsewhere. Her work has been nominated for a Pushcart Prize and several times for the Best of the Net. She currently lives in Princeton, New Jersey. Find her at: https://shannonkwinston.com/

Glass Lyre Press

exceptional works to replenish the spirit

Glass Lyre Press is an independent literary publisher interested in technically accomplished, stylistically distinct, and original work. Glass Lyre seeks diverse writers that possess a dynamic aesthetic and an ability to emotionally and intellectually engage a wide audience of readers.

Glass Lyre's vision is to connect the world through language and art. We hope to expand the scope of poetry and short fiction for the general reader through exceptionally well-written books, which evoke emotion, provide insight, and resonate with the human spirit.

Poetry Collections
Poetry Chapbooks
Select Short & Flash Fiction
Anthologies

www.GlassLyrePress.com

CPSIA information can be obtained
at www.ICGtesting.com
Printed in the USA
BVHW070234131021
618791BV00004B/63